T0197428

KARTER: This is Me

Crystal Shivers

AuthorHouse™
1663 Liberty Drive
Bloomington, IN 47403
www.authorhouse.com
Phone: 833-262-8899

This book is printed on acid-free paper.

ISBN: 978-1-6655-6646-9 (sc)
ISBN: 978-1-6655-6645-2 (e)

Library of Congress Control Number: 2022913993

Print information available on the last page.

Published by AuthorHouse 07/26/2022

authorHOUSE®

Dedication

Dedicated to my daughter Karter (My Suga). Her drive to achieve her dreams at such a young age and her wonderful spirit are what inspires me everyday. Mommy loves you.

Hello, I'm Karter with a K. Come on and read what I have to say.

When I was born I was a preemie, which means I was born early. Though the day was scary, my parents were so excited to meet their beautiful little girl.

I finally got to leave the hospital after a week and a day. Mommy had to wait patiently because she knew before she took me home they had to make sure I was okay.

From there life seemed to be normal and I grew up so fast. Before we all knew it a whole year had passed.

I learned to walk, I played and I tumbled. I loved to be silly and I tried to talk but I just mumbled. Soon my parents noticed how much I fumbled.

I walked a little crooked and I always walked on my left toes. When it didn't get any better it was time to go to the doctor they supposed.

So to the doctor we went and the news made mommy and daddy cry. I sat there confused because I didn't know why.

OMG MY BRAIN!

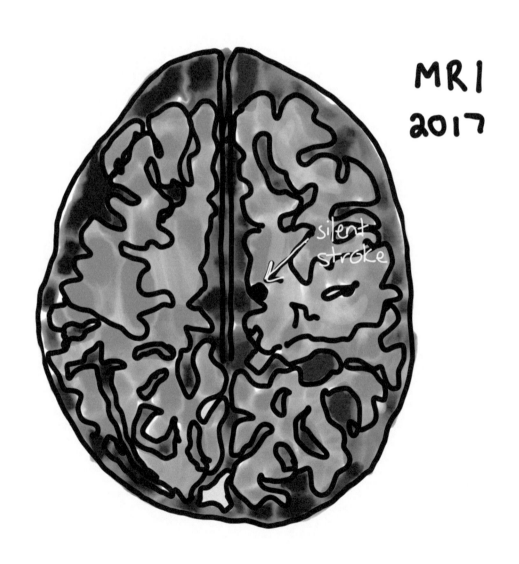

MRI
2017

It turns out that when I was in my mommies tummy I had something that they call a stroke. When my parents heard this, it's why their hearts broke.

The stroke caused nerve damage on my left side of my brain, which is why I would fall. I was diagnosed with something called Cerebral Palsy, an MRI made that final call.

Though my parents were sad, the doctors knew just what to do. They gave me a brace to help me walk, and I even had surgery too.

The brace helped me walk and the surgery helped me run. Now I have the confidence to never be outdone.

I can be a gymnast, a runner, or anything I put my mind to. Especially because I have mommy and daddy to help me through and through.

When I grow up I want to be a doctor. Maybe I'll work in sports and help my cousin that wants to play soccer.

I am smart, energetic, I love to swim and I love being goofy. And even though I have Cerebral Palsy, I know that the days to come will never be too gloomy.

So if you're like me, don't be scared, be brave. I make progress everyday with the situation I was gave.

With the love and support of my parents and family I have come a very long way. I know that as long as I have them I will always be okay.

Printed in the United States
by Baker & Taylor Publisher Services